Fruit Mansion

Dear Jen,

New friend! Hello! Thank you so much for buying the small, fruity lil book! I hope you enjoy your first AWP and I look forward to being real life friends and internet friends! ☺

♡ Sam

Fruit Mansion

poems

Sam Herschel Wein

Sam Wein

Split Lip Press

Published by Split Lip Press
333 Sinkler Road
Wyncote, PA 19095
www.splitlippress.com

ISBN: 978-1978397415

Cover Art by Anya Liao
http://www.yovngcoconut.com/

Table of Contents

Teething

Take the split of a cantaloupe,
rip it clean off
the rind, rub it in salt
& tar &
tie a string behind a roadbike, count pieces of
gravel afterward in its smile.
that is a dead boy on the
news, see how animated the anchors
& their hands
make him a scene,
digitized & on a screen &
in a coffin
cantaloupe is a fleshy fruit for
people like you, obsessed with
death. the first time you
ate it you dipped it in ketchup & everyone
screamed
about it in your mouth, not the
blood, shallow drip
down your chin, *Sam dipped fruit
into ketchup*
but the juice
dried & within you,
family joke for years

knife party

on aisle three,
kraft macaroni & cheese next to isle grown
potatoes, children who poop where
the mop can't reach,
the fuck we supposed to do
when the stores close, anyway,
said 24 hours
before *thank you for shopping,*
goodbye convention of time
units, so the toilet seats cracked,
so the extra hour snapped
our knuckles,
the inflated balls all popped
and none of the sweatshirts
were neon, guys, *come on*
just this once, grab a weapon &
carve into the golf clubs
or anything metal
enough for this to break
us.

clean up
on aisle seven,
knife party
with three wounded,
superstores that don't run
on hours anymore because
businessmen couldn't
spare the wages
the store workers couldn't breathe
but everyone's *gone,* you know?
called it partying to cover
the bleeding
like the cops with their guns
aimed at barrels, or kids, or small
town folk,
damaged goods
unnoticed both in & out the store,

knife party in every aisle,
last one standing gets the broken mirror,
slide its cracked frame down
the back stairs and pray that the shards
stay put.

Angst in Threes

White knuckles clenched. Playground boys run. They don't stop. Kissing in
kindergarten. Kissing in third-grade. Use the tongue. Against the wall.
Everything is pressed. Naked at sleepovers. Naked in attics. Naked in
basements. Everything is sex. I never asked. I television watched. I
actor / actress. I the part. I playing stage. He smiles, bites. Indented,
bare arms. Nobody calls home. Not even thirteen. Summer camp friends.
Jewish school friends. Tennis court friends. One after another. Pinned against
me. Everyone is naked. Just so young. Just so hungry. How was school? My
little mathematician? I learning angles. Geometry of bodies.

I not sleeping. The house,
silent. I awake, alone.

Growing a Boy

How does a wrist bone grow to hold the size of a tree?
Once, unable to grapple the loop of a pacifier?

How does oldest sister take the news? Is it
on the cob? No extra butter?
I am eating anything my lips can hold, parents say
I *must*, I am *growing boy*—
sister is older girl, sister not
a twirl of steps, sister not a body parents like
so she doesn't get to eat all that I do.

                                              no one tells her it's

wrong
the extra helping on my plate

                                              no one tells me

to stop
parents that ladle masculinity

                                              and everyone takes a

bite of
me, I loved the spoons
fattening me, then
peeling me large from the inside

but no one told my sister she could too—
so she didn't, but did,
but I was thick-necked boy and growing
but she was girl put on fifth diet
since middle school
dance photos

and it shouldn't be a surprise
the phone call last week

Sam
I
feel
so
small,

hand the spoon of a phone to my mother,
say here, say you fed us something that's
made us all sick.

First Nights

I lay in bed, a hotel
room in Canada, a twelve
year old boy sleeps without
waking next to me. I am
also twelve, & pudgy. Hips
round. The boy in the bed
sleeps like a coiled snail,
a wound up spaghetti
noodle on a fork,
taking up more than half
the space. I realize
I am struck
by his bottom, the way it
is plush and on my leg, I
am an oven on fire or
a hot pepper eaten
unexpectedly. My body
presses entirely against
his, symbiotic.
I stay up all night
like this, I do.
We wake up, he winces,
we touching, conjoined
curvature, he broken for the
bathroom not asking if
I've slept well or at all.
No, I would like
to say, the light
from the window exposing
flapping skin
No, I would like to
scream, sheets splayed
in air 10 stories high like a
winded tongue, I'm wrapping the
lamps like ghosts
to see if they, too, are able to
shine while being simultaneously
unable to breathe
you look so
tired, another friend
says. *Were you out*

all night? A secret
agent? Tell me about your
double life.

essay on eating picture frames

joint with couch cushions, collaging colors
balance each other in,
inside picture frames
are dribbles of paint for mourners, or criers, or depressed
you, you swallow the frame whole
and watch it collide
with wooden stomach floors, an art gallery
of disappearance
I can tell you now, this isn't an

essay on your mother in law, your
overweight uncle, the dog that died,
already three summers ago? seems
like yesterday was essay
on breaking up on his mattress, did you
read that one? your own
words? trace it into the bottom
of the sink? break the
drain, swing around
the pipes?
could've sworn it was

essay on overpriced carpets,
pillows of stuffing for every foot,
foot of the table that's crooked with
misused words
falling over
no one wants to eat dinner
without it
but the family broke all
its legs, I guess, the table
split to pretend trees, hexagonal shards
like its design, plastic bark
a metaphor for losing
something or an

essay on a family's loss
told by me, the entertainer, the one
who writes and cries and is

consistently the most yelled at
consistently yelling
the most.

For Barney

"It doesn't matter if you're Black, Gay, or even Purple, we must all unite…"
— Some gay CEO on the news

I pledge allegiance to the black, gay, & the
purple, & the white gay men in the high-rise

buildings among waveless waters & politicians
whose speeches hover above knees over gravel

buzzing like broiling sausages & I pledge
allegiance to Barney, violet scales, leafy green

belly bumps, I pledge to the country of Barney
& gays & blacks & minorities in speeches or

cardboard sayings or one identity-fits-all or one
identity-fits-none & purple next to my identity

like it's as alive as I am & gays of power or really
business white gays pledge allegiance to green,

green, & green & this country that wraps legs
with flags that trip us when we run to protect our

selves & this is about purple & possibly purple
is a successful ode to those settling here & always

this country's legacy; someone's identity is unable
to come & if I am like the purple, the rainbow's

inside, the bottom wrung, do I, indignant, blame
the blues & yellows for not held down a hand?

I remember Barney called for family, & Barney a
guitar of songs on how to love with a whole heart

& singing, on key, *family is most likely to witness
bleeding of its members* but the white gay family

doesn't see this & it's all purple or bust & white
people all have one thing in common, all love to

call the police & I think I would like Barney if I
met him now, though I meet him every day, like

at protests, lost beneath the mayor's thumb,
hidden in book burnings, but in sleep, they ask

me to forget, forget, he doesn't exist, written in
rest & the cardboard shreds.

Fruit Shopping

Middle of the party, just starting
to dance, he said,
"are you a pineapple or an asparagus?"
but the music was too loud to
hear him, so I asked him to speak up,
though I could read his agape
lips. Was he asking about
my thorned personality, prickly and obtuse?
Was I shriveled at an end– too smart?
His eyes beckon to his crotch, my eyes
rainbow posters on the wall,
left temple parallel to the floor.
I think if I were a fruit I'd be
a passion fruit,
I think I'm a wild artichoke, I think I kiss
people harder than others– but that's
a secret. His eyes
on me waiting for a response,
my mouth circling my head tilting his
hands pressing my legs I said well I
whispered I ate a banana this morning,
I hush hushed that guavas grow in tropical
climates, wanting to scream that pineapples
go from loose to tightly brimmed pants
with boots, pineapples aren't asparagus
but they do shrivel
& get lost & get felt up at parties
without offering permission.
"Are you a fruit or not?" his hands
reached for my inner thigh, & I
tried to say, I'm
not ready
to be splattered seeds, I'm not
ready to pick or be picked.

How to enjoy wine tasting

You are an incomplete ice sculpture. He slides his other hand down your back.

sip

Your front door, home alone and he was there tapping gunshots on the wood, how you were bleeding out a lung when your eyes caught in the peephole, the neighbors all helicopters shining lights on him at your porch, an investigation he begged the papers to report.

swirl

The dance, the jazz band, all of your friends dressed in oversized suits. You, wearing your father's dress shoes. You had just finished swing dancing with a girl in a green, floating dress, when his hand clinched a forest bird on your shoulder.

pour

Remember 16, both an age and temperature you hate, how you wanted everyone to look at you, swirling a pencil on your desk, hours on youtube learning to dance, practicing an organic smile sweet as an heirloom tomato. You wanted an orchestra set on lilypads, water swaying at each step.

gulp

Smell the shampoo, how after swim practice he would squirt it on you as boys piled like tentacles into the showers, and he would wink. None of them blinked. How he would wait for you, the slow dresser, in the hallway, and the days you were the last one, you wouldn't find your way home from the wall of his chest and the wetness always left on your neck.

Leave your legacy at the door

because I don't give a fuck
about it. My mother calls me
again about my poems, how
her extended cousin found
one, & in it, I mentioned sex
with a boy on the swim team.
And? My phone smells of
lecture & coffee beans. My
notepad in my arms feels
like a war machine, like
a flag stuck through planets
to shatter them. *Your legacy
is all you have in this world.*
I'm sure you think that, Mom,
I'm sure you thought that
when asking my sisters, both
of them, if their husbands
would still be interested in
them once learning about
their *gay brother,* your
legacy brimming with pride
as you thought about moving
cities, your son had come
out & you, only worried
your friends would find out.
Mother. I'm upset, in grief.
One poem inappropriate
for a cousin does not outlaw
the ones filling their window-
gardens with musings &
mustard seeds, we are in
constant planting of handles
& gripped, dangling by scarves
on some road, together. Believe
in this, how the lampshades
illuminate us, could outshine
our ancestors. We are holding
hands in the roller rink,
gliding away from
the walls. I'll fall first.

I am a breakfast sandwich

Oblong, tepid breadloafs,
O hole in me round as an egg-
shell. I am galvanized to thick
creamery, I am soggy with
overnight dew. He takes one
look & thinks, *deformed*. He
takes one bite & screams, *I'm
swollen*! & I am shipment to the
factory again, a breakfast
psychologist muses, *why can't
people swallow you whole,
swallow you at all?* and I wonder
why people don't chew their
food like their teeth are wilted
like I'm to blame that they
lose their smiles

but it's morning, it was evening,
some holy day, some grace &
blessing, tongues of the world
wake up & I say, hey, thanks,
thanks for joining the sun today,
I think it's happy we're all here,
though another man in a white coat
explains *I'm not a real bagel*
anyway, my wheat, veins, pressed
thin as rice, hole, heart, just frameless,
looping steps,

here I am, dancing at breakfast, tidal
waves of caffeine-free battery blood,
energizer orange, ornery ocean, circling—
how many pinkies, I wonder, could fit,
right there, on me? I'll keep adding 'til
I am crumbs, 'til no spine, no yeasty rise.
O bagel, o me. O broken arc. How I
wanted an egg salad sea, how the fish
already smoked and no one offered me
a hit, O ocean. Tainted, but vast.

Sailing on Tuesday

She built molten ships with rotten arugula from the store,
celestial towers run amok through an overly damp sea

& who watches the hold, anyway, who captains the
refrigerator with its plug alone on the wood, the food

warmer & warmer every day like summer. She empty,
the arugula wet like sink-turned towlettes, the ship a

bridge beyond her ocean countertops & lighthouse
towered walls, she sat & watched green sail from her

nails like a seaweed sunset. A handful left in her left
palm, a mermaid folded into a clam, a pirate so fierce

he bedazzled his peg-leg, stamped a crystal on his eye-
patch. What is the ocean if not an exile exonerated?

What could be more glorifying than living atop
a green sea, a salad spinning tornado, a tomato-less

haven wet as grape seeds? Each leaf fell from her
to an open trash, not bothering to board with a ticket,

no wristbands for seasickness on their stems. She
put the ship away by its hull, slinking each flag &

sail stich by stich under her shirt, the arugula a
missing fountain, overturned airwaves, lost as sea.

Asking for Sugar

Pink grapefruits,
preciously sweet, a sharp-
edged spoon that is pressure
beyond what the skin can
take; *I wanna fuck you*
so bad he snarls behind my
gums, his mind a pink
pasty flower gritted
to no petals at
all, my mind a pain like
bitter coffee or consuming
cigarettes whole to see
if nicotine works in the stomach
too. It didn't. I didn't
teeth his white lace seeds,
didn't squeeze any skin 'til juice
dropped in the bowl,
I didn't ask for sugar or spit or
anything
smooth to guide the taste
down something small, sour
stinging on every nerve, vitamins
lost like
my body is
supposed to swallow everything
whole. At breakfast, I can't
eat the fruit out the too
white bowl, a pink so plush
its palpable and pain-
ridden past, *take it you*
little pussy a mantra for fruits
and breakfast fruits
and cigarettes that don't
taste like smoke anymore
that don't taste like
I can eat anymore.

Hey Fat Boy

Bet you can't eat just one.
cylinder cement slabs
table legs
bet if you were less monster,
less sasquatch & body hair
bet if you saw your love on the street—
the tables rolling over the hill
        with no legs,
wonder if tasted you could have been
sweeter, wonder if English
you could have better spoke,
wonder if you were less man of cave,
less chin drizzled, hand eating chicken bone

bet if he asked you to be skinny, *boy*,
if he pulled
at your sides, needled a trampoline,
bet you would stop eating the arms
off the chair 'cuz you were still
hungry, the napkins hurled afterwards
        out of shame,
bet you would be a mouse in the
stairwell of your love,
bet you couldn't have asked
for anything, or seconds,
        or a piece of cheese.

bet you thought you wasted all that time
over him, & getting over him, like it didn't
press the petals to fall,
bet the seasons didn't stop for you like
you asked them to,
his lips
mid-word & your mind, a mouse
scurrying under every foot
in the city,
waiting for scraps
to fall.

Hot Dogs

"Hot dogs are so phallic!" I yell
through the wall. "Uh huh," he says
back, not looking up. "He doesn't
understand," I bemoan to the roasting
broccoli florets, "he's too straight!"
Like every roommate I've had. All
these hot dog eating straight men
I share dinners with, who needs them?
I wonder if he would squirm at me
walking by his door, a cucumber
dangling between my legs. I wonder
how he attacks a breadstick. I won-
der if the cannoli drips on his face
if he's concerned. Carrot, banana
ingesting boys I live with, maybe it's
me, maybe I'm more gay than they
want, or need, but how can they
look at me with those eyes when
they eat a Stromboli with those lips?
filling and all? sauce staining their
shirt? I wonder if I had a gay room-
mate, would we eat the hot dogs
staring into each other's mouths?
Would we dive to catch the ketchup
before it hit the floor? Would we
lick it up? "People aren't like that in
real life," my roommate calls back
from the other room. "I don't see a
vagina in any of the foods I eat." I
scoff at this, like he thinks about
anything besides his majestic rod,
coughing, snorting, asking him how
many historical architects, builders,
designers, were women, how many
foods I've eaten besides a restaurant
flower share the anatomy of a female
crotch, as if worldly designs resemble
much else besides hot dogs, the male
euphoria, the Eiffel tower poster in his
room blooming off the wall, unrelenting
as a pickle

Pulling Teeth

a boy does not
cry Wolf.
you think Wolf isn't as sharp as desk
edge? you
think Wolf isn't grandmother eating, basket
swallowing,
broken glass in the home, serrating the light?
I tried,
just once. bellowed a bomb big as my broken
lip, I said to
the woman how he teethed and tattered my empty
shell. she said
back, "oh, *boy*, that's just how he is. I'm sure he didn't
mean it that
way. you let him take off your clothes? you thought
it wouldn't
get anywhere? don't go turning this into a game, *boy*,
this school
does not approve of those who cry—" but I opened my
mouth to finish
her off, the sentence of her, my paw on her nose scraping
clean layers
of skin until I could see what large teeth she had, *my, my,*
what pearls,
what ivory filling the chairs in every room at once.

Holiday

Here is your lesbian orange
my cousin plops the orange on
the cream tablecloth directly
in front of me, forming a dent
in the fruit. I take hold of the
orange with green, neon nail
polish. It's holiday season,
one of nine, Jewish families
gather around square tables &
an extra table stood up at the
end: "the kid's table," where
I sit at twenty-three. Earlier
that night, mid-Seder, I read
an old tale of placing an orange
on Seder plates to commem-
orate gay & lesbian Jews that
escaped from Egypt & slavery
& current oppression within our
communities. *Rabbis still refuse
to speak of our existence!* I am
arms circling in dead air. My
parents bat their eyelashes.
My aunt sneezes right on the
word "lesbian." My best friend
growing up's parents look
concerned to their youngest
son, only 16. Does he know
about the gays yet? & he'll
hear it like this? My voice
wavers, I stumble saying the
words "we are not yet free." I
wish, while reading, I had said,
"freedom is relative, we just
forgotten, we arms outstretched
held beneath the table, finger
imprints missing on our invisible
skin." Her fingers hold for a second
on the orange. I am back sweat &
clicking nails. *Say it's brave, say
I did something good, say anything,
please.* She heads into the kitchen.

I leave my house the next day, hug
my parents goodbye & don't hesitate
when pulling out the driveway.

Ode to Cheesy Potatoes with Uncooked Onions

I'm lying on the floor curled like an L to
fit on two rugs, one of them smells of feet
and feces. My stomach, a swordfight poked
and punctured. I scream, "You onions!" as if
somehow, inside me, they *intentionally*
become millions of mini knives, thrown
haphazardly. Earlier, I had balanced bites in with
the Chinese takeout and the Lactaid pill I took,
all on a roommate's used plate, still reeking of
crusted, reheated cheese. I recall, now, that onions
had once sent me to an emergency room, thought
I had an ulcer, but the doctor said "slight trouble
with digestion." Here I am, two AM, startled
awake by you hardened in me, scraping linings,
my burning insides. I'm lying on the bathroom
floor, both ends are a two sided-tea kettle,
hot to touch. I wallow, sing a choked man's
song. I try to scream again but poop, rather, in
my underwear, sideways still on the bathroom
floor. I sit up, start vomiting. I think back to one
of my good friends, moved to Chicago same time
as me, but with a partner, they live together. She
said, "I got so sick, I passed out on the floor,
completely shit myself. My partner had to carry
me, shit and all, to the bathtub. I can't imagine
what I'd done if she hadn't been there," *but I
can*, I was alone at four AM and I crawled into
the shower, scrubbed underwear while heaving
to ward off the nausea. I looked like a broken
horse, nose caught in the drain. I couldn't
distinguish my tears from the falling water, both
too clear to lap in my hands, my hooves, my
arching spine. After the shower, I threw up every
cheesy potato I'd eaten. After the shower, I took
the first forty minute nap since my first run to the
bathroom. I woke up and threw up again, shat
in my pants again, until my friend showed up at
ten AM with some ginger ale and crackers.
"Fuck food poisoning," I said, gently. Be
gentle, I thought, I made it, no partner and I
made it, no arm around me and I made it, shaking

to not pass out from the pain and I made it, first
bite of banana down and I made it, sipping soda,
stomach a whirlpool still, bathroom an estranged
smell still, but I made it, I made it, I made
it.

Please Place Your Masks Over Your Mouths

I'm eating the cupcake you gave me
& scribbling notes to my first ever work-

friend, Brenda. Brenda is a very focused
worker so I scribble her notes to ask if

she wants to have lunch, convinced
that notes are less distracting than my

voice. I'm all askew. I'm a turnaround
town. The cupcake crumbs smudge

frosting onto an important work
document & I gaze over the wording,

wonder, *what makes this doc*
more important than my grapefruit

sex poem? Both font & print, both
trying to change someone's life? You

give cupcakes for my birthday
& yell, again, for me to come to

your office. *Sam! You've been*
doing great, enjoy today on me!

& you placing a hand in a grip
firm & on my bicep & it slides a tiny

bit up my arm & I'm back at my
desk creating more crumbs writing

office-friend Brenda more notes as
she works as I'm writing he keeps

TOUCHING me he keeps asking
about my goddamn SEX LIFE &

Brenda eats her burrito at Chipotle every
bite is ricebeanslettuce is mouth full

& crowded taking bites instead of
Sam maybe you should say something
but everyone's breathing & not
telling me that so maybe the oxygen's

too damn free that no one is willing to
point out the crumbs spreading from

my fingers like a wildfire & in my
beard & my desk chair just so many

cupcakes I'm an eatery my friends an
airplane oxygen mask applied to

themselves before looking to see if
others need help.

Invisible Whale

Tell me about the network television program where
he slid closed my cabinet
drawers, etched with a pocket
knife our initials under the sink. Tell me about the ocean
he dove into among two
squids, a clam without its shell,
and how the crabs swirled tornadoes, each clamped onto
fingers and toes. Read me
a script, how he left me alone on a fishing raft,
a motor boat, a single hanging tree above
a green, forgotten sea. Tell me about the time he painted
a mural of me on the old
bank downtown, no one stopped
to ask him for his name, or mine, he drawing the arch
in my back so publicly, I felt
the colors in my pores. Tell me this, all
this, has been somewhere
for me to watch. If not,
quick, start to film. Get out the camera. Say
that I too can exist in pixels
and on eggshells, that my
love and I can try to be seen together. Do not tell
me to wait. Do not tell me to patience.
Show me the time he fell so in love with
the idea of me, he hijacked
a newsroom, took over
Channel 6, colored in an invisible whale
and held it up for the police, smiling.

How to Cook Your Family

Look, under the meat cleaver, a painting
of my grandmother grows plants for us
to breathe, feeds from the light in the
golden, sparkling wall. See it there? Six
full cows hang in a row in the freezer by
the back. Isn't this what you always dreamed
of? From five years old, slogging with wet
shoes, holding a stuffed Torah? What we
waded through, survived for? Not this kitchen—
but lava from an old volcano, the doomsday
campaigns stuck in our nostrils, then us, leaving
the ridge, elevated to watch it pass by, feel
its warmth, and live; that's what this is: chip
in the golden, sparkling, rainforest wall. Family
obsessed with genocide, but only of its own
demise, of one lens history, family portraits
like tilled earth beneath our toes. Bring me
a chicken coup. Bring roller skates for us to
dance in. Sprinkle the rays, disco the fire,
collide, bleed, blossom, all beyond our
grubby fingers. We don't see where we're
going, why would we look, now? We stumble,
broken the metal oven. We pray now on the chip,
the ray, so delicate and silver on a spoon. You,
kid. Child of dimness. Take the whisk, an open
faced loaf, journey for more light, let us know
when you've found it, please.

Waiting to Pop

I wanted this to be a water balloon.
What's this? He asks, so I untie a
shoestring from my lungs, drag
it all the way to his hands. I say,
I want to drown, I say, this wet
cactus, this scaling skin, let's blow
this joint, take me out. *What on earth,*
he gasps, steps away from me
like I am a bomb, like he'll feel
shrapnel sooner than he's ready.
I try to pull the shoestring myself,
but it becomes licorice at my touch,
I can't stop salivating and he's
shaking in the corner, praying.
I don't want your prayers,
I try to scream through candy
lungs, sweetness abound. I walk
over to him and vomit. It falls like
crystalline, smells like citrus. I
feel acidic, but not toxic. He can't
die off me, I decide, he can't
handle me at my worst,
he doesn't deserve me at my
innocuous, at my pepper spraying
bandits, I say, I can't do this, you're
inconsolable, I drape a coat over
him and begin to leave. *Wait!* He
barks. *Don't let the violence
get to you,* he's pleading, *you are
careening, you might blossom.*
I say, this is what violence does.
It stays with a person. It's every
new cut I've gotten since, it's the
sharpness in my neck most mornings.
It's everlasting. You, I want to say,
are not. But I don't say much after that.
He hugs me, and I take him home, and
when he nibbles a moon in my back,
I want to die again, but choke on
his fingers, stay lightheaded.

Tongue to Tongue Cool

We were on the inner tube, you were in 8th grade.
You said *Sam* with a voice meant to inform me I
was doing something annoying. I looked over and
you pushed me off the tube, head first, the water
crashing my ears to my ankles, my feet flailing to

flip myself and come up for air. Our parents rushed
over, concerned. I bobbed below the raft, not yet
ready to pull myself back on. Or maybe it didn't
happen this way, this time. I can't remember. I was
only eight. We were on the tube and I was wet.

You said *Sam* in the voice you often use for our other
sister, the one we would pick on. You said *Sam* and
I turned and you asked if I knew what a "French kiss"
was, and I thought of the French, of their chariots and
their cheeses, I said "no" but really I was thinking

about French fries and lunch sides. You explained
about tongues, our parents had went upstairs and
the water was a hazy speckled green and the raft
was blue or red but definitely round and you said
here you said *let's try it* and we touched our tongues

it tasted like saliva? it tasted like the smell of dad's
hairbrush, it tasted like when I slept on your pillow
one time and I must have made a face because you
pulled away and said we wouldn't tell anyone and,
until this, I haven't. Until this, it's been sunk as the

old raft, the metal one we would jump off, or unvisited
like the island we tried to canoe to and got stuck
halfway with no further arm strength, dragged by
jetski back to Grandmother's house on the lake. The
next year, I date a girl from school, tell her I learned it

somewhere special, she says none of her friends have
heard of it. I am nine years old, she is pressed against
a wall, I am pressed against her hair, and
I am tongue to tongue cool, I am talk to tongue cool,
I am talk to classmates about the tongue cool, I am

classmates with their tongues hidden behind their
throats cool, but then I tried to be tongue to tongue
in the boys bathroom with my best friend cool, his
lips for a second soft as the inside of a book, but I
was tongue to the wall with his hand grabbing my

hair nerd, I was his hand raising my arm so high I
thought it would break nerd, I became boy other boys
don't talk to unless needed in sports nerd, because I
could play sports, because I could play tongues, because
tongues are slippery, wet, because my body forgot to

breathe under the raft, because my limbs are fickle
and could maneuver in and
out of any mouth, in and
out of any mouth
I pleased.

What the Mansion Could Look Like

for Ian

What I'm trying
to say is: the fruit mansion is a circle of
hanging lights, a
perpetual crisp wind bringing summer
to a close. We are
all illuminated. None of us exploit one
another. I am trying
to say the fruit mansion still stands
abandoned on
Manchester, in the first gay bar I set
two feet in. Look,
it's rotting on California Ave., lost in
translation on
Halsted. I'm saying this mansion needs
some tools, a
set of compassion and callused hands,
that our
safe haven is infiltrated and burning.
I'm trying to say
the mansion is only as wealthy as its
inhabitants' hearts,
we don't need size or a house that looks
like the rest
for it to be beautiful. That we, all of us,
flood every
vacant home to the brim, we uncontained,
we not constrained,
clasping hands at breakfast and daring
each streetlight
lick our connected skin, I know queer
families look
like pomegranates insides, bunched
seeds that seep
fingers in holding, in ceremony, this, us,
a miracle,
a crown of pineapples atop our heads.

Acknowledgements

I want to thank the journals and magazines that have published my poems & believed in me as an emerging writer.

Construction Literary Magazine: "Teething" & "Leave your legacy at the door"
decomP: "Invisible Whale"
Gabby Journal: "Fruit Shopping"
Mobius Magazine: The Journal of Social Change: "Knife Party"
New Plains Review: "Asking for Sugar"
No Assholes Literary Magazine: "What the Mansion Could Look Like"
PANK: "Tongue to Tongue Cool"
Pretty Owl Poetry: "Hey Fat Boy"
Red Paint Hill: "Sailing on Tuesday"
TL;DR Magazine: "essay on eating picture frames ," "Angst in Threes," & "For Barney"

For instilling in me the love of writing, I would like to thank Kathleen Finneran, Adam Segal, Jacqui Germain, & Eileen G'Sell. For encouraging me to find my voice & helping me to develop my craft, my immense thanks to Julia Kolchinsky Dasbach & Talya Zax. To my most avid readers, my thanks to Emily Jungmin Yoon, Tyler Tsay, Maya Jewell Zeller, Joshua Aiken, & Kris Tavassoli.

For spending hours on the phone debating the queerest words, for reading to me on Facetime the many poets whose work inspired me, for believing in me with every step, my thanks & my love to Chen Chen. For holding me up, & being the family I needed while working on this chapbook, my love & gratitude to Amie Soudien, V Chaudhry, Mia Salamone, Anya Liao, Madison Cannon, Kate Harrington-Rosen, Elena Coronado-Jensen, Caroline Burney, Alison Tune, Taylor Nys, Susie Bernero, & Ari Esienstadt. For teaching me how to follow my dreams, my endless thanks to my dear, beloved friend, Ian Harris Schroeder.

For selecting this work & helping it become a reality, my thanks to Amanda Miska, Cyn Vargas, & the team at *Split Lip Press.* To the communities of writers who have supported me, I want to thank the team at *The Blueshift Journal* & the team at *Construction Literary Magazine.*

To my sisters, for always loving the person that I am. To my grandparents, who I wish I could have shared this with. To my parents, who have watched my growth, & have supported & loved me through all of it.

To every young queer person who feels like the loneliness will never stop. To a scared, depressed, younger version of myself. Thank you, with my whole heart, for holding on, for making it here. Thank you for not giving up.

ABOUT THE AUTHOR

Sam Herschel Wein lives in Chicago and specializes in aimless frolicking. He is a poetry editor for *The Blueshift Journal* and is co-founder of a new journal, *Underblong*. Recent work has appeared in *Vinyl Poetry, Pretty Owl Poetry*, and *Connotation Press*, among others. See what he's up to at **shmoowrites.com**.

NOW AVAILABLE FROM

Split Lip Press

Felt in the Jaw: Stories
by Kristen N. Arnett

Gather Us Up and Bring Us Home
by Shasta Grant

Antlers in Space and Other Common Phenomena
essays by Melissa Wiley

I Once Met You But You Were Dead
by SJ Sindu

Plastic Vodka Bottle Sleepover
by Mila Jaroniec

Because I Wanted to Write You a Pop Song
by Kara Vernor

For more info about the press and our titles, please visit:

WEBSITE: www.splitlippress.com
TWITTER: @splitlippress

Made in the USA
San Bernardino, CA
01 November 2018